LOOKING AT LITERATURE

MY FIRST LOOK AT FAIRY TALES

BY ROSIE BANKS

Gareth Stevens PUBLISHING

Please visit our website, www.garethstevens.com. For a free color catalog of all our high-quality books, call toll free 1-800-542-2595 or fax 1-877-542-2596.

Library of Congress Cataloging-in-Publication Data

Names: Banks, Rosie, 1978- author.
Title: My first look at fairy tales / Rosie Banks.
Description: New York : Gareth Stevens Publishing, 2022. | Series: Looking at literature | Includes index and webology. | Audience: Grades 2-3
Identifiers: LCCN 2020028215 (print) | LCCN 2020028216 (ebook) | ISBN 9781538263952 (library binding) | ISBN 9781538263938 (paperback) | ISBN 9781538263945 (set) | ISBN 9781538263969 (ebook)
Subjects: LCSH: Fairy tales–History and criticism–Juvenile literature. | Tales–History and criticism–Juvenile literature.
Classification: LCC PN3437 .B36 2022 (print) | LCC PN3437 (ebook) | DDC 398.2–dc23
LC record available at https://lccn.loc.gov/2020028215
LC ebook record available at https://lccn.loc.gov/2020028216

Published in 2022 by
Gareth Stevens Publishing
111 East 14th Street, Suite 349
New York, NY 10003

Designer: Rachel Rising
Editor: Kate Mikoley

Photo credits: Cover, p.1 Larissa Kulik/Shutterstock.com; pp. 3, 4, 6, 8, 10, 12, 14, 16, 18, 20, 21, 22, 23, 24 (background) carduus/DigitalVision Vectors/Getty Images; p. 5 Colin Anderson/Photographer's Choice RF/Getty Images; pp. 7, 9 Pobytov/DigitalVision Vectors/Getty Images; p. 11 Thomas Barwick/DigitalVision/Getty Images; p. 12 Culture Club/ Hulton Archive/Getty Images; p. 13 Imgorthand/E+/Getty Images; p. 14 clu/DigitalVision Vectors/ Getty Images; p. 15 ZU_09/DigitalVision Vectors/Getty Images; p. 16 Grafissimo/DigitalVision Vectors/Getty Images; p. 17 duncan1890/DigitalVision Vectors/Getty Images; p. 19 Historical Picture Archive/Corbis Historical/ Getty Images; p. 20 Miguel Navarro/ DigitalVision/Getty Images; p. 21 pkline/E+/Getty Images.

Printed in the United States of America

CPSIA compliance information: Batch #CSGS22: For further information contact Gareth Stevens, New York, New York at 1-800-542-2595.

CONTENTS

Boldface words appear in the glossary.

Magical Tales

Fairy tales are a part of growing up. Parents and teachers often read fairy tales to children. Fairy tales have been made into books, TV shows, and movies too. What makes a fairy tale different from other kinds of stories? It's magic!

Not Just Fairies

Not all fairy tales have **fairies** in them. However, they all have a bit of magic. They might have witches, elves, giants, or other **fictional** kinds of characters. Events often happen in these stories that couldn't happen in real life.

Fairy tales share **features** other than magic and magical beings. They're often about a past time. They may be set in a castle, forest, or **kingdom**. It's usually easy to tell who is good and bad. Most teach a lesson and have a happy ending.

Old Stories

Some fairy tales are thousands of years old! At first, they weren't written. People told them to each other. Later, people began writing them down. The stories weren't just for children. Some were written for adults. Many were scary!

Storytellers

Hundreds of years ago, people began gathering fairy tales. They put them in books for others to read. In the late 1600s, French writer Charles Perrault wrote a book of children's fairy tales. It included "Little Red Riding Hood" and "The Sleeping Beauty."

Charles Perrault

"Little Red Riding Hood"

In the early 1800s, German brothers Jacob and Wilhelm Grimm **published** books of fairy tales. They collected more than 200 tales in all. They changed some stories. Sometimes they added lessons. "Snow White," "Rumpelstiltskin," and "Rapunzel" are a few famous Grimm fairy tales.

Grimm brothers

"Snow White"

Hans Christian Andersen was a storyteller from Denmark. In the 1800s, he wrote 168 fairy tales. His most famous are "The Ugly Duckling," "The Little Mermaid," and "The Princess and the Pea." He wrote the stories like he was telling them out loud.

Hans Christian Andersen

"The Little Mermaid"

Changing Stories

Stories change with retellings. Charles Perrault and the Grimm brothers wrote different Cinderella stories. This story goes as far back as the 800s in China, though. In a **version** from Italy, Cinderella's stepsisters cut off parts of their feet to fit into her slipper!

"Cinderella"

Fairy Tales Today

People today study fairy tales. These stories can tell us what was important to **cultures**, such as kindness, cleverness, and good **behavior**. People haven't stopped writing fairy tales. New ones are still published. Try writing your own fairy tale!

Your Turn!

Think of your favorite fairy tale characters. What event might get them to come together? Write a short fairy tale. Read it to someone!

GLOSSARY

behavior: the way someone acts

culture: a group of people with the same beliefs and ways of life

fairy: a creature that looks like a very small person, is magic, and sometimes has wings

feature: an interesting or important part

fictional: made up or not real

kingdom: a country whose ruler is a king or queen

publish: to produce a book for sale

version: a form of something that is different from others

FOR MORE INFORMATION

BOOKS

Colfer, Chris. *A Treasury of Classic Fairy Tales*. New York, NY: Little, Brown and Company, 2016.

Minden, Cecilia, and Kate Roth. *Writing a Fairy Tale*. Ann Arbor, MI: Cherry Lake Publishing, 2020.

Wu, Faye-Lynn, translator. *Mulan: The Legend of the Woman Warrior*. New York, NY: Harper, 2019.

WEBSITES

Fairy Tale Stories for Kids
www.kidsgen.com/fables_and_fairytales/
Here are some easy-to-read fairy tales.

The Grimm Brothers' Children's and Household Tales
www.pitt.edu/~dash/grimmtales.html
Read tales that the Grimm brothers collected.

INDEX